Episcopal
Is
Compelling

Published by
Saint Alban's Episcopal Church
1803 N. Gold Point Circle
P. O. Box 1104
Hixson, Tennessee 37343

Stanzas 3 and 4 from the hymn "God My Father, Loving Me" by G. W. Briggs (1875-1959) used by permission of Oxford University Press.

Quote from "Santa Claus Is Comin' To Town" by Haven Gillespie and J. Fred Coots. Copyright © 1934 by Leo Feist, Inc. All rights reserved. Used by permission.

Excerpt from ON BEING A CHRISTIAN by Hans Kung. Copyright © 1976 by Doubleday & Company, Inc. Reprinted by permission of Doubleday & Company, Inc.

ISBN   0-9606174-0-X

Library of Congress Catalogue Card
No. 81-50931

First Printing September, 1981
Second Printing April, 1982
Third Printing November, 1984
Fourth Printing June, 1986
Fifth Printing July, 1987

*To the Glory of God
and in thanksgiving for
Lynn Chapin Patten,
my very special saint.*

Saint Alban's Day
A.D. 1981

CONTENTS

Preface

The reader is captured by the reality that pervades Father Patten's statement of what the Christian Faith and the Church mean to him in this presentation of basic Christianity as held and practiced by the Episcopal Church. He is a parish priest whose ministry has been marked with power and effectiveness in assisting others in their personal journey in faith and in bringing the three congregations he has served to great spiritual vitality and strength. Both this little book and Father Patten's ministry reveal the essential quality of a spiritual leader and pastor - the willingness to offer one's self in such openness and candor that he speaks persuasively to the mind and heart of others. In this book, he gives the reader a candid glimpse into his personal convictions and presents in an intriguingly personal and novel style the faith and traditions of the Church he serves and loves. The reader will find this a helpful introduction to some of the characteristics of the Episcopal Church and, beyond that, find Father Patten a delightful companion with whom to share one's personal journey in faith.

+ *William Evan Sanders*
Bishop of East Tennessee

1. Places to Start

As a life-long Episcopalian and now as a parish priest, I feel somehow called to attempt a short, informal, non-technical reflection on key points about this Church I love. Its message, its approach to love and life, its rich traditions, all widely misunderstood, have peculiar power and potential for giving hope and new life. The Episcopal Church is in an unusual position in our mixed-up, frustrating, complex world to be the bearer of new meaning, new truth, new wholeness, new fulfillment to those of God's children who are in spiritual need, who hunger and thirst for Him.

There are already many books on this subject. They are authored by scholars and theologians much more learned and articulate than I. I want to admit that I feel a little presumptuous in making this effort. The justification for this is that my approach will be somewhat different, more pastoral, and less academic. As a matter of fact, I have done no special research in preparation. What I am writing comes off the top of my head in the light of my experiences and training as an Episcopalian, a priest, and a human being.

My hope is that this book, while serving as an open, down-to-earth introduction, might also be helpful in classes for adults who are considering joining the Episcopal Church. I want to deal with key concepts, the basics, but not in over-powering depth. For those wanting to go further, there are many excellent books. My aim is to keep these remarks simple yet well-rounded and reasonably complete.

In talking seriously about the Church, one first needs to try to be clear about Christianity. There are many different understandings, often conflicting. We cannot assume "Christianity" means the same thing to both of us. However, it is my experience that my own understanding does not differ importantly from that of educated clergy of other Christian churches (Baptist, Methodist, Presbyterian, Roman Catholic, etc.). We have more similarities than differences. Good, main-line seminaries today are teaching just about the same thing.

However, some of my clergy friends in other denominations seem not permitted to teach or preach the faith that is theirs. It appears to me that for this and other reasons laymen may come to understand that one brand of Christianity is "right" while another is "wrong." As I have said, this is not the feeling among the clergy I have known from other "main line" denominations. But I have experienced a communication problem in the case of some of their laymen. Therefore, it is important that I try to make clear my own understanding which I take to be acceptable, not only in Episcopal circles, but by informed members of all major Christian denominations. Among them the emphases may vary and the outward and visible things do differ, but the basic message, the Good News of God in Christ, seems similar to me.

Misconceptions have crept in. Many people have been turned off because of poor communication and untrained teaching which have led to inappropriate expectations. For these reasons, I hope not only to express my view of the Episcopal Church, but also something of my understanding of Christianity. I am a Christian first, an Episcopalian second.

The question that confronts me now is, "Where should I start?" The whole matter is like a closed circle. There is no logical beginning point. So, we simply have to dive in somewhere and go round the circle. Hopefully it will all come together at the end.

It must be added, for the reader's soul's health, that one's spiritual pilgrimage is never complete in this world. There is always more to experience, deeper levels to know: (Jesus Himself said He did not know everything. Mt. 24:36.) Anyone who thinks he has arrived, who has found a comfortable place to sink his roots, who feels called to go no further in the Christian quest, is selling himself and God rather short.

Therefore, it needs to be understood that what I propose in these pages are only first, beginning steps. One may be tempted in either of two directions: 1) To see this short effort as complete and full and enough. Sorry! There is much, much more. You can't in good conscience stop here. 2) To view this presentation as too childish, too incomplete, lacking in too many areas, and reject the whole bit.

So I remind you it is meant to be only a beginning, but a *solid* beginning. I hope it is a thoughtful starting point, an adequate foundation for further discussion and deeper inquiry into the mysteries and power of Christianity from a specifically Episcopal point of view.

It needs to be said here at the outset, and as strongly as possible, that one cannot possibly hope to come to an understanding of the Episcopal Church without attending the regular Sunday services for several weeks - six to eight, anyway. The order of service, the ritual, the sermons, the music, the people are all an integral part of coming to understand. If you have never been to one of our services, it may seem strange and awkward to you at first. By the third time you should begin to feel more comfortable and from then on, increasingly so.

Come a little early. Sit quietly and think or pray. Relax. Really give your cares to God as you open your heart to Him. The quiet dignity of the service is one thing new people appreciate. The Episcopal Church, like God, must be personally experienced, not just read about, to be known.

Finally, three more brief remarks before I end this introductory chapter.

It used to bother me as a boy to hear priests I greatly admired say from the pulpit such things as, *"We* are all sinners." I thought to myself, "Surely *he* isn't a sinner. He's just saying that to make us feel better." It seemed sort of patronizing to me. Now I know better. We are *all* sinners, including us priests. I haven't arrived either. I am a pilgrim, too. Let there be no mistake about that.

Second, I don't mean to be a male chauvinist, although I must admit I did come out of such a culture. Whenever I use the words "man" or "men," I mean "mankind," both men and women. I'm growing, but I'm still not altogether comfortable with "person." However, I do enjoy the new postperson who serves us.

Third, if you sincerely want the most out of this book, you will find it extremely helpful to obtain a copy of *The Book of Common Prayer*[1] (1976 or 1979 model) in which to follow the references I will be making. All Episcopal Churches will be glad to lend you one or tell you where you can buy a copy.

2. The Need

Everything I can think of that has worth exists to fill a need. The family, government, schools, sports, picture shows, artists, rescue squads, weather forecasters, nursery rhymes, fairy tales, and most everything else meet definite needs. What is the human need that keeps the Church in business? Until we experience the need for her, the Church cannot have meaning for us.

It used to be that the Church existed to save us from the "eternal fires of hell." Preachers scared people into shaping up and into supporting the Church. "You'd better watch out, you'd better not cry, you'd better be good, I'm telling you why,"[2] referred at one time not to Santa Claus but to God. Religion and the Church were for dying and going to heaven.

For as long as I can remember this has seemed a right selfish approach. "I am to be good so I can go to heaven and not to hell" sounded somehow unchristian. Over the years I have come to the firm conviction that Christianity is about life and living rather than just *earning* life after death. There is plenty of New Testament material to support this. So I have decided I will leave to God what happens to me after physical death. I believe in God, and I believe He loves me. It is my faith that God will see about me and you when we depart this life.

The needs I have for the Church are of this world. I notice something is basically wrong with me. With St. Paul, I find the good I would do I am not able to do and the bad I really don't want to do is exactly what I do. (Romans 7:15). I lose "my cool" sometimes. Often I am not content with my job and my life. I get in ruts and get depressed. I don't take as good care of my body as I would like. My pride gets me in trouble. There are other things, too. They all add up to the clear fact that I need some powerful, down-to-earth help: not psychiatric help, I think, and not medical help. The help I need is of a different kind. For me to live life to the full, to experience heaven on earth rather than hell, to know now what Jesus called the Kingdom, I know I need *special* help.

I have noticed that other people need help, too. There are lots of serious, personal problems around. The sky-rocketing divorce rate and all the sorrow this brings is only one example. How about the phenomenal abuse of drugs in our culture? So many seem tired, bored, and lonely - life has lost its spark nothing to look forward to. Too many lives are spent unhappily in just taking up time with no meaningful purpose. Obviously, something is bad wrong. There is a deep-seated need for a new day, a new life, new strength, new vision, new hope.

Much bigger than my own needs and those of lots of people I know is the sickness of the entire human race. When millions of Jews are murdered in World War II, when torture is practiced world-wide, when so many are starving, when there is such wide-spread suffering, there just has to be something wrong ... bad wrong.

Others have noticed this besides me. Over the years many answers have been suggested and tried. But not a single one has worked. There have been political answers, sociological answers, economic answers, and others. They hardly scratch the surface!

When it is all added together - my need, the needs of the people I know, and the infinite needs of millions I don't know - we are plainly in a mess. It's not just me - it's everybody.

Some people, particularly Americans, are apt to say, "If people would just get to work and stop moaning and groaning everything would be OK; willpower, discipline, and hard work are all we need." This is the so-called

"Puritan Work Ethic" to which we Americans have fallen heir. History has proven this doesn't work either. Not only does it not work, but it makes people feel guilty because they can't pick themselves up by their own bootstraps - like Paul said. Things like child labor, slavery, prejudice, pride, and unbridled power keep it from working. We are too greedy, too stingy. It is possible for someone on top of the heap to talk about hard work being the answer. But this is of no help at all to children caught in the ghettos of degenerating cities. Such children are trapped.

As a matter of fact, when you think about it seriously, it becomes clear that just about everybody is trapped in one way or another. Nobody in his natural state is really free to be what he was created to be. We are all condemned to being less than we could be. For example, no one knows very much; we are trapped by our ignorance. Not many people give very much; we are trapped by our selfishness. We are trapped by the false values of our schools and cultures. For instance, we are pointed toward "success" which means "doing well," "making money," "being popular," "becoming a star," "marrying well," etc. These are the kinds of worldly goals that trap us, sap our energy.

The Bible has a very ugly word for the cause of all of us being trapped and in such a mess. We don't like that word: SIN. Like a disease, it infects us and makes us sick. It seeks to defeat us, destroy us. It is so real that it seems to be a separate, outside thing that has come over us like a demon or a devil. It is like a gigantic spider web or a morass of quicksand. It gobbles people up both from the outside and inside. Everybody is infected by it. We aren't sure where it comes from, but that makes no difference. It is a sorry fact of life and living. It is SIN in which we are all trapped. It is SIN that has made for one horrible mess within me, within lots of others and throughout the world.

This is not to say that people aren't good. To the contrary, I am convinced they are basically good. If I weren't good, if I didn't have good ideals, I wouldn't particularly care about my life, about my wife and children, my neighbors, or the world. But I do care, very much. And most other people, except maybe a few, seem to care. We are good enough to care, so we aren't all bad. And, too, we are good enough to try, to want to do something about our situation.

As I have said, we come up with answers, but they don't work. We make New Year's resolutions, take vows, read self-improvement books, and take courses. Many people do try. No, we are not all bad by a long shot. It's just that we are sick and can't help ourselves.

And this is what the Church is about. It was founded to meet the need for a cure of our sickness. This is why the Church exists. It has been said, "The Church is a hospital for sinners, not a country club for saints." The Church exists to give you and me and the whole world a way out of the defeating web in which we are so strangely caught.

If you think you are OK, maybe you don't need the Church. Perhaps the Church is not for everybody. I know two or three really fine people who do much good and who seem very happy, but who aren't in the Church. Maybe that's OK ... maybe. But of one thing I am sure: it makes no sense to be a part of the Church unless you want to improve the quality of your own life or the lives of others. So, if your life is already fulfilling and exciting, if you are fully satisfied with things as they are, if you find yourself in solid touch with *ultimate meaning,* then you may not have the need for which the Church exists. If you want to find new life, new goals, new hope, new freedom, re-creation, then you are looking in the right direction because this is what the Church is for.

There are, of course, other reasons for the Church. It can be helpful and supportive as we face the crises and tragedies of life, the mysteries of life, the mystery that is life. It can help meet our need for friends and society. And then, we might say that the Church exists to meet some needs that God has, but this is getting a bit deeper than I intend.

I have suggested that the Church is the answer to my slavery to sin and the slavery of the human race to this same power. "But," you say, "this hasn't worked either." The best answer I know to that is, "Indeed it has worked wherever it has been seriously tried." Countless lives down through the centuries attest to this fact.

Or you might say, "Well, that sounds great, but it's a far cry from any experience of the Church *I've ever had.*" That's OK, just keep reading. My hope is that things will be very different for you this time. The Episcopal Church offers something special in its approach, and many people have had no acquaintance with it.

This is a good place to say that it is not

necessary or important for you to agree with me. That's one thing I love about my Church. I can be me, and you can be you, and we can be solidly together with our differences. This makes for a rich association, a depth we wouldn't have if everybody was exactly the same, thought the same things, had the same ideas. In this free exchange, you will help me and I just might be able to help you a little, too. And together, under God, we will help no telling how many others.

3. The Language of Love

Somewhere near the beginning, like right now, one thing needs strong emphasis: many things just aren't what they appear to be. This is especially true of language and devastatingly true of religious words.

It is imperative to distinguish between two radically different kinds of language, called *sign* and *symbol*. A *sign* is simple and direct. It means only one thing. "Stop!" is a sign. It means exactly what it says and no more than that. "$1 + 1 = 2$" is also a sign. It is to be interpreted literally. Much arithmetic and science use signs. To drive a car or fly an airplane we must understand and obey all kinds of signs. To make a good Strawberry-Chocolate Torte I would have to follow the signs in a recipe carefully and literally. In addition, signs aren't very interesting.

In our culture, through our schools, and because of our fascination with machines and elementary sciences, we have been led to believe that substantially all language is sign language. Our first thought is apt to be that everything can be figured out, proven or disproven, logically. We might even argue that if something can't be figured out, it ought to be changed or discarded entirely as useless and meaningless. We surely have an overpowering, dominant tendency to approach everything in terms of "1 + 1 = 2." And in doing so, it seems to me, we may be missing something like 75% of life and living.

Because, you see, there is a second kind of language which is infinitely more powerful and meaningful than simple, boring signs. This is the language of love, of art, of spirit, of hope, of faith. This kind of language is called *symbol*. Unlike *signs*, *symbols* have many meanings, often inexhaustible. They are far from simple. They point beyond themselves but also have within them at least a bit of that something to which they point. They are much more alive and interesting than signs.

There are countless examples of symbols. Some may be more powerful for you than others. I hope I can pick one for which you have a feel. (Note: we never have a "feel" for signs, unless a sign has become a symbol for us.) Let's try the American flag. Everyone knows that the flag is only some colored cloth sewn together in a certain design. For me, the American flag is a powerful symbol. As a boy I was taught to handle it with care, never let it touch the ground, fold it correctly, not let it get wet. You would have thought it was holy or precious or something and should cost a lot more than $24.95. In standing for my country, it stood for lots of things: for my hopes for myself, for power, for goodness, for freedom, for love, for blood, for honor and for much more. And if somebody tore down the flag and set it on fire, for me much more than cloth was being burned because a symbol contains in itself a very part of that for which it stands.

For some today the flag has lost power as a symbol. We can add, then, that symbols can become empty and meaningless. Misuse or disuse destroys them. For example, many things in the Church which used to be symbols have for some degenerated into signs -like the cross.

Let's try another. A mother goes into her little boy's room, tucks him in, and kisses him goodnight. On the one hand, this is simply a series of plain, mechanical actions of no material worth. Human lips brushing a human cheek. A hand touching another hand. The power in this symbolic action goes well beyond logic. Should the mother ever refuse this symbol, her son might cry all night.

Look at yourself in the mirror. What you see, your body, is a symbol. It is not the real you. Cut off an arm or a leg, and the real you has not been diminished although its symbol has been changed. Where are *you* in that body of yours? Sometimes you wash it, shave parts of it, and dress it nicely, and this says a good deal symbolically about you, does it not? Your actions are symbols, too, of the real you. Clearly, they are not you, but they speak of you and somehow are a part of you, or you of them.

We could go on and on. Wedding rings. Homes. Clerical collars. Our cars. Light. Clothes. Personal letters and phone calls. Money is an especially deep and powerful symbol. All of these are clearly in a different class than simple signs.

The language of love is symbolic since love cannot be described directly and literally. Poetry is poetry mainly because it uses symbolic language:

> *In Xanadu did Kubla Khan*
> *A stately pleasure-dome decree*
> *Where Alph, the sacred river, ran*
> *Through caverns measureless to man*
> *Down to a sunless sea.*

—Coleridge

Can you tell what this means? That is the wrong question. A better one is, "Can you tell some of the things these lines mean to you?" Obviously it is not like "Stop!" or "1 + 1 = 2." Many people don't like poetry (or classical music) because, they say, they can't understand it. Then we need to ask what they mean by "understand." Was it meant to be understood in the way they imagine? The problem, I would suggest, is treating a symbol as though it were a sign and that just doesn't work. It's an "apples and oranges" proposition. Poetry is to be appreciated as a symbol which probably means one thing to me, something else to you, and has an entirely different meaning for the author.

Thinking seriously about these things makes it clear (and a little scary) that the most important things in life can only be talked about through symbols. Signs won't do when it comes to love, beauty, hope, spirit, faith, and all the other things that really matter. And so it is that when we get to religion, we'd better watch out. If we approach its language, as is our bent, as though it were sign language we are in trouble - just like we are with poetry and with love. Religious language is mainly symbolic. Take the word "God" for example. That word is a symbol and not a sign. It speaks of many things: life, death, ultimate meaning, creativity, judgment, to name just a few. We are even warn ed not to use God's name in vain because to use His name in improper ways is to use Him in improper ways. This symbol, like the others, contains in itself something of that to which it points - like the flag. All the important things are communicated by symbols, and faith is not the least of these.

We have already hit one such word: SIN. This is a symbol. It helps to think about and discuss what this symbol means to you. One thing for sure, it is not a pretty symbol because what it points to is ugly, not pretty. The ancient *Kyrie,* "O Lamb of God, that taketh away the sins of the world,"[3] is a symbolic expression of belief. To try to see it as a simple sign is to miss the point.

The Church has an important word that points to a special kind of symbol. It is *sacrament*. One definition of a sacrament is "an outward and visible sign of inward and spiritual things." This is an important concept for Episcopalians which we will look at in some depth as we go along.

In this understanding, the world is a sacrament (or symbol) of God. He made it out of nothing. He sustains it. It is His. It is different from Him, yet He is in it. It stands to reason that when God wants to communicate to us in His world He might well do so in a sacramental way. There would be an outward and visible part to carry the inward, invisible, spiritual part. He did this in Jesus of Nazareth whom we say is a sacrament of God. The Church uses many symbols to describe this reality: Son of God, Word made flesh, Good Shepherd, Savior, Lamb of God, the Christ, to name only a few. Each of these attempts to communicate the belief that God Himself was in Jesus of Nazareth reconciling the world to Himself, that Jesus is God - both God and man.

It follows that the Church is a sacrament of Jesus Christ. We say the Church "is the Body of which Jesus Christ is the Head and all baptized people are members."[4] It is both a physical body and a spiritual body. It has outward and visible parts which carry inward, hidden, spiritual parts, like your body and mine.

In the Church there are seven services which we also call sacraments. Baptism is one of them, established by Jesus Himself. The outward and visible parts are water and certain, set words. Surely, we believe, Jesus would not command us to do this if it had only its outward side. Like Jesus Himself and like the Church, the outward and visible signs of Baptism carry hidden, spiritual power.

Among them are cleansing, reconciliation, dedication, empowerment, becoming a member of the Body of Christ (the Church). He whom we believe to be God-in-man said to do it. We, the Church, do it in the faith that it has important, essential gifts for us and for the world.

He similarly instituted the service of Holy Communion. At a supper, He took bread, thanked God for it, broke it, and gave it to His disciples saying, "This is my body which is given for you. Do this in remembrance of me." Then He took the cup of wine and passed it to them saying, "This is my blood of the new agreement between God and man." These are plainly outward and visible things, bread and wine and certain words. He said these elements were His body and blood. What did He mean? At the least, we believe He meant there was something very special about bread and wine when taken in this way, in His Name. The outward parts of this sacrament carry within them powerful, invisible, spiritual gifts from God who knows our needs even before we ask.

Summing up, little in this world is just a simple sign. What you see of me with your eyes is only skin deep. My body is a symbol of the real me and much I do is symbolic. Since the most important things of life can only be communicated in and through symbols, I have to agree that God communicates with you and me through symbols. And so it is that I can experience something of God in a beautiful sunset or a flower, in another person or in myself, in a work of art or even in a mathematical expression. These are all symbols of Him. And He came to earth in a symbol, Jesus Christ, who established a symbol of His continued presence, the Church, which in turn, incorporates numerous symbols, some of which are known officially as sacraments.

I have tried to show it is essential in religion to measure all things on the sign-symbol yardstick or we will be fooled and miss the point. Is the story of the feeding of the 5,000 a sign or a symbol? How about Jesus' turning water into wine? St. John's Gospel calls them "signs" (John 2:11). Does John mean by "signs" what I have meant in this chapter?

How about the Second Coming, the Virgin Birth, Adam and Eve, the parting of the Red Sea, the Transfiguration, Judgment Day, and so many other things? Are these literal $1 + 1 = 2$ signs or are they deep symbols? Some Episcopalians go one way and others another. And I like that about my Church: I am free to think and choose for myself. And as I am freed to choose, I am freed to be me.

Finally, on the subject of religious language, it will be helpful to consider one more technical word. The word is *myth*. Its everyday, usual meaning is "not true" or "made up." *This is not the sense in which it is used here.* Because of this confusion, I wish we had some other word to use, but we don't.

Its technical, religious definition is "a myth is a true story about the relationship between God and man which may or may not be historical."[5] The power of the story is in its truth about God and man's present relationship, not in the story's historical validity. What is important is what the story says about me and God now, today, and how what it says bounces off my own experiences.

For example, the Adam and Eve story is a *myth* in this technical sense. It says many things including that God made me and you and we goofed and that God still cares. Whether or not there really was an historical Adam and Eve is obviously not anywhere near as important as the basic truths this story relates, truths that apply directly to you and to me today. A myth, then, has some of the powerful properties of a symbol. Some of Jesus' parables are like this, too. The Parable of the Prodigal Son is only a story, but the truth it carries rings with unearthly power.

As we go forward, please keep in mind the distinctions between *sign* and *symbol* and this special, technical meaning of *myth*. They are all important in the language of religion, in the language of love, and in the language of just about everything else that really matters.

Please be aware, too, as you begin to attend our services, of the many *symbol* words that are used and of the symbolic actions you will see. There are *signs,* too. It is helpful to recognize the difference.

4. The Story

Because this chapter contains a lot of symbolic language, you will find it more interesting than some other chapters. Let us begin.

When I was a boy, I learned from my father a little nonsense story you may have heard:

It was a dark and dismal night.
Around the campfire were seated brigands large and brigands small.
The Captain, addressing his trusty lieutenant said, "Antonio, tell us a story."
Antonio arose and spoke as follows:

EET VAS UN DARK UND DEESMAL NIGHT.
AROUND ZEE CAMPFIRE VERE SEATED BREEGANDS LARGE UND BREEGANDS SMALL.
ZEE CAP-A-TAN, ADDRESSING HEZ TRUSTY LIEUTENANT SADE, "ANTONIO, TELL US A STORY."
ANTONIO AROSE UND SPOKE AS FOLLOWS:

…it was a dark…and a dismal…night.

...around the campfire...were seated
   brigands...large...and brigands...small...

My Dad would continue for a long time.
With each rendition, Antonio would have a
different voice: loud or gruff, accented one
way and then another, falsetto, high drama,
simplistic, stammering, etc. We were always
delighted.
   Our life together in the Church is like that.
This is because our life together is centered on
a story which we tell and retell again and
again. We tell it in different ways with different emphases. We not only tell The Story
continuously, but we act it out in the service
of Holy Communion and at other times. The
sermons comment on it, as do the hymns,
psalms, prayers, and just about everything
else. We are story-centered.
   Outside church, as we live out our lives, we
continue to act out parts of The Story
-sometimes one part, sometimes another. As
a matter of rather startling fact, The Story
that the Church tells and retells is, in the final
analysis, your story and mine. This may seem
like a rather strange and remarkable statement. It is!
   The Story has, over the years, been greatly
adorned - artistically, dramatically, sym

bolically, and in other ways. Some say it has been overlaid with unnecessary dogmas, doctrines, traditions, and practices which only muddy The Story, making it hard to recognize and understand. If this is true, it is too bad, because actually it is a simple, plain story that even a child can understand. In the technical sense it is a *myth* (a true story about the relationship between God and man that may or may not be historical). It goes like this:

Once upon a time there was a person whose name was Yahweh.[6] He lived in the highest of places above all heavens. One day, for reasons of his own, Yahweh began a mighty work. He fashioned from nothing the entire universe and all that is in it - the sky, the stars, the whole world.

Yahweh gave his special attention to a small bit of his creation called Earth. Here he planted all kinds of trees and shrubs, grasses and flowers. And he caused to spring forth on Earth all manner of sea life, birds, insects, and animals, all in rich variety. He put in these living creatures a governing force called instinct which enabled them to live and have their being without even thinking.

When all else was ready, Yahweh introduced on Earth a completely different kind of creature called Man. Yahweh made Man male and female and in his own image. He gave Man a body like animals and some of the same instincts which were to insure Man's physical survival. But Man was not created to be governed by instincts as were the other creatures.

Instead, Yahweh gave Man a mind with which to think, a heart with which to care and love, and a soul so he would know he was part of a bigger enterprise than just what he could see. Specially equipped as he was with heart, mind, and soul. Man was given an important job by Yahweh: to take care of Earth and all the other creatures who lived there.

Very early in the game, something seemed to go wrong. We can't be sure if things really "went wrong" or if this was the way Yahweh had planned it all along. Anyway, as it turned out, instead of using his heart, mind, and soul to look after the rest of creation for Yahweh and to be Yahweh's special friend, Man used his mind to fulfill his animal instincts. He used his heart less and less to care and love, his soul less and less to talk with Yahweh and know about bigger things.

This trend of more and more instinct and less and less heart and soul snowballed at what seems to us to have been an alarming rate. Parents, knowing less and less about heart and soul, taught their children less. And so it was Man ended up a strange breed, interested mainly in the fulfillment of his now greatly expanded instinct-demands. For example, his instinct for shelter turned into a desire to own giant mansions and castles at all costs. And his instinct to eat led to his building up of world-wide empires.

As a result, Man cut himself off from Yahweh, becoming chronically unhappy, dissatisfied, strangely lonely, frustrated. It came to pass that when a new baby was born it simply didn't have a chance to be what Yahweh intended. The whole human race ended up in a deep pit - a mire of quicksand from which Man, no matter how hard he tried, could not escape.

Yahweh, of course, knew about this turn of events - if it really was a "turn" of events. From time to time, he raised up men, sometimes called prophets, who spoke of better things, of a new way, but they could not be heard or followed in the circumstances that now existed.

Then, in what might appear to be a last resort kind of effort, he chose to befriend a special people...an insignificant, untalented group of slaves. He worked especially hard with them, freeing them from their bondage and promising them their own land and many good things if they would be close to him like Man was made to be. But they, too, like an unfaithful spouse, sought the fulfillment of their badly warped instincts. Man was too hardened, too conditioned, too far away from the world of heart and soul, too bound into the visible world.

It became an unbelievable, seemingly hopeless, madman's world. In his guilt and frustration, Man even turned boldly against Yahweh, his creator, for allowing such things to happen. They said things like, "How can a loving father do this to us?" (This, obviously, is the wrong question, completely missing the point.)

Yahweh was patient and when the time was right, he came to Earth himself in a man, born of a human mother. In the eyes of the world, this man was most insignificant. Even his family found him embarrassing. Instead of urging the further fulfillment of raw instincts like everybody else wanted, this strange man called for a return to the world of heart and soul. He knew Man was trapped, actually enslaved, and could not free himself. "Follow me," he said, "and I will get you out of the quicksand, out of the deep pit, into the kind of life you are meant to be living. Believe me, there is no other way for you to escape. You are too far gone to ever save yourself.''

As could have been easily predicted, the world at first completely rejected this man. He was killed, as even he knew he would be. He gave himself for Man, for Man's salvation. No one seems to know for sure exactly how his giving of himself in this way might save Man. But many people later came to agree that he did to the full whatever was necessary so that Man could be saved from himself and united once again with Yahweh.

To make this point absolutely clear and unmistakable, Yahweh raised this man from the dead. No other fact of ancient history is as well attested to as that one. This part of the myth is stunningly historical. Of course, no one understands it all except Yahweh, but it is not necessary for Man to understand it completely. In and through this man Yahweh did all he could do, all he can ever do, all he needs to do, to rescue Man.

Some few people then banded together to take this man seriously. As he had promised, he sent what he called his Spirit to guide and strengthen them on their journey from the way of raw instinct into the way of heart and soul. Against overwhelming odds, this little band grew by leaps and bounds. It came to be called the Church, the Body of Christ, which is mightily empowered by his Spirit. Through the Church, his Body, the voice and Spirit of that man who was killed and raised again from the dead is still heard loud and clear, "Turn and follow me, and I will take you to your true home." He has come to be called the Savior, the Good Shepherd, and Lord.

That is basically The Story the Church tells and retells. There are many other parts that add to it, like Yahweh's chosen people wandering around in the desert for 40 years. The stories of Noah and the Ark, of the mighty King David, of blundering, blustering Peter, of Paul's great faith, and many more add to The Story, giving it great depth and living power.

The really funny thing about The Story and what makes it so interesting is that it is also my story and yours. I am Adam in the Garden of Eden eating the forbidden apple, kicked out never to be admitted there again. I am Cain killing my brother Abel, David lusting after Bathsheba. I am Hosea's unfaithful wife. I am the writer of many of the psalms. I am Abraham and Moses whom God called. And I am Jacob who was not faithful but who inherited the promise anyway. I, too, wander in the wilderness, and sometimes I get to high mountains where I can be still and know that "thou art God." Yes, the more I think about it, the more I see that The Story is my story. And I confidently submit that it is your story, too.

Like our stories, yours and mine, it is an unfinished story. The myth is projected on into the future. This special man will return. The Kingdom of Yahweh will arrive on Earth in all its fullness, and things will indeed be as Yahweh first had in mind. This means that, come what may, you and I and everybody else will become what God intended. He made us free. And He will wait, gently prodding, until we choose the Way, the Truth and the Light He has given us...the *only* way out of the mess we are in.

It might be helpful to pause a minute here and consider what parts of The Story are simple signs and which are attractive and interesting symbols. Do you feel the mystery and excitement of it all? Is there for you in The Story a ring of eternal beauty, truth, and goodness, a sense of being called to what you were created to be? Can you sort of feel your own slavery and glimpse the freedom that for you is like the Promised Land? Do you feel inadequate and unworthy like Moses did, or like the miserable little band of slaves in Egypt, or perhaps like Mary, Peter, or Paul? What do you make of the coincidences between The Story and yours? As you experience The Story in and through your own story, doesn't The Story seem more and more true? A true story about the relationship between God and Man.

5. *The Roots*

(Since this chapter contains a lot of *sign* language, it might not be as interesting to you as some of the others. But it is not devoid of *symbol.)*

Because we are what we have eaten and have done and have thought, we are, in fact, our past. This is true of us individually, collectively, culturally, and in other ways. Although it is surely our task, our calling under God, to change and to grow, we have to begin where we are as a product of our past. As it is with us, so it is with the Church as a whole and with the Episcopal Church in particular.

Episcopalians are one part of the worldwide *Anglican Communion* now number over 100 million people and at the moment growing most rapidly in Africa. The Anglican Communion is a voluntary association of independent national churches all of which have the same roots. The *Archbishop of Canterbury* in England, by tradition and continuing consensus agreement, is the "convener" of the Anglican Communion. He is the symbol of our common roots. He has no specific authority over the Episcopal church or any other member churches, unless they be in England or are missionary arms of the Church of England.

churches, unless they be in England or are missionary arms of the Church of England.

That is what we are. Now, how did this come about?

In the third, fourth, and fifth centuries The Church spread miraculously. (This, in itself, is powerful and convincing testimony to the power of the Spirit that is in the Church.) The Roman Empire governed most of the "known world," and the Church quickly moved into all areas of the Roman Empire and beyond. By the second century, bishops (overseers) were being set up as head pastors in towns and cities everywhere. St. Paul mentions them in some of his letters. It made sense for Paul and other missionaries to put someone in charge when the Church was started in a new town.

In the third, fourth and fifth centuries, these bishops met together in important councils. As can be easily understood from the political situation, in the course of time the Bishop of Rome became a sort of "first among equals" and then a kind of "head bishop" and, finally, the Pope. The rise of the papacy is, in itself, an interesting story. We only note here that the Bishop of Rome eventually became the Pope with authority over the Church wherever it was located, or at least in most places. We shall mention shortly one place where the early Popes did not have authority.

Around the year 1000 A.D., the Eastern Orthodox Church, headquartered in Constantinople, broke away from the Western Church which was centered in Rome. This was the first major split in Christendom. The grounds were partly political, partly doctrinal, partly cultural, and included such things as the "right" date for Easter.

Long before this split, the Church had spread to what is now England. Nobody knows how it got there, although lots of intriguing legends have come down to us. There are records of three English bishops attending councils in Europe as early as 314 A.D. Other written records indicate a considerable colony of believers in Britain by 200 A.D. I happen to be serving a church named for St. Alban, the first British martyr who was executed around 209 A.D.[7]

In 586 A.D. a monk, who was to become Pope Gregory the Great, visited the slave market in Rome. He noticed a group of attractive, blond, fair-skinned youths. He called them "angels" and asked where they were from. The slave-master told him they were from some large islands off the coast of northwest Europe (i.e. Britain). In 597 this good Pope dispatched one St. Augustine (not to be confused with the more famous Augustine of Hippo) to these islands to convert the "angels."

When Augustine arrived, he found the Church there ahead of him, as we have noted above. In fact, the king's wife was a Christian. Augustine worked effectively to spread the Church in England and to consolidate its efforts. Eventually a working alliance was struck between the Church in England and the Church in Rome. Over the years that followed, the English Church was sometimes solidly in the Pope's camp but often not. The English were a proud and independent people. Some strong English kings rebelled against the Pope. Weaker ones kowtowed to Rome. And there were many shades of allegiance in between.

By the late middle ages, the papacy had entered a period of considerable decline, complete with the kind of corruption to which power leads. Meanwhile, the Age of Enlightenment dawned over Europe with such powerful discoveries as the printing press and the appropriateness of reason. When the German priest Martin Luther suggested some reforms of the Church in 1517, he unwittingly lit a fire which still roars today. The Protestant Reformation was begun. Such new denominations as Baptist, Presbyterian and Lutheran were born.

But at this time in England, things seemed reasonably calm on the surface. There was a good deal of discussion of the reforms taking place on the continent, and a few people were burned at the stake for seeking to initiate reform. King Henry VIII denounced Luther and was given the title "Defender of the Faith" by the Pope. This title is still attached to the English crown.

Then it happened that Henry wanted his son-less marriage to Katherine of Aragon annulled by the Pope. This was a usual and regular practice, normally causing no problem for kings and other politically powerful figures. But on this occasion, the Pope was a virtual prisoner of Emperor Charles who was the nephew of the queen Henry wished to shed. Charles was not about to let the Pope harm his dear Aunt Katherine. So, the Pope, under duress, said "no" to Henry. Thereupon, Henry backed by reformers who had caught the bug from Europe, replied. "You go by your way, and I'll go mine." The Church in England was the same as before: same priests, same bishops, same services, same everything – just no allout allegiance to the Pope any more, if there ever really had been such an allegiance.

Henry died in 1547. His son by a later marriage, Edward VI, became king. Only a boy and sickly at that, Edward was controlled by strong reformers, and the English Church swung far into the Protestant camp.

When the boy-king Edward died in 1553, Henry's daughter became the monarch. She was staunchly Roman Catholic and promptly returned the Church in England to the Roman fold. She repaired the overt split of Henry and became known as "Bloody Mary" for her severe persecution of the reformers who had blossomed under Edward.

Back and forth went the English Church as, it seems to me, it had always done beneath the surface. Then came Queen Elizabeth. She formulated a "middle way" (Latin: *via media*) which has characterized the Anglican Communion ever since. She and her advisors set out to preserve the most worthy of the old traditions, incorporate the best thought of the reformers, and establish once and for all a church structure that was both faithful to the past and viable for the foreseeable future.

An important part of this story is the work of Henry's Archbishop, Thomas Cranmer.

After broad studies of Christendom's forms of worship, he compiled *The Book of Common Prayer,* said to be the second most influential book in the English language. The first edition came off the presses in 1549, under Edward. (Cranmer, refusing to support Mary's return to Rome, was burned at the stake. His is a brave and tragic story.)

The Church of England also translated the Bible into English, the King James version coming out in 1611. The system of having bishops in Apostolic Succession (see below) was retained along with many former customs and traditions. But the Church was freed up, made more like it was in the beginning, while retaining good and helpful additions from the heritage. The strong sacramental emphasis was preserved. Bible reading and prayers in the language of the people were adopted. Clergy were allowed to marry. It was a beautiful blending and remains so.

The Church of England was taken to all corners of the British Empire: Hong Kong, India, Africa, Australia - everywhere the British flag was raised. It came to Virginia with the Jamestown settlers and to Georgia with Oglethorpe. It spread through the 13 colonies. But later, as one could well imagine, there were considerable problems because of the American Revolution against England. To start with, there were no bishops in the American colonies, and it takes a bishop to ordain priests. Also priests of the Church of England were required to vow allegiance to the English throne.

In spite of the turmoil, the Church survived in the United States. It became a new, national Anglican Church - as far as I know the second one, after England. It was originally called *The Protestant Episcopal Church in the United States (PECUSA)*. But now it is just *The Episcopal Church.* Episcopal (from the Greek *episcopas:* overseer, bishop) means "having bishops" (see chapter 8). Our church remains allied in spirit and heritage with our mother Church in England but is in all ways fully independent.

In addition to the *via media* stance set rolling by Queen Elizabeth, there are other distinguishing marks of Anglican Churches. There has always been a freedom for open inquiry, a latitude in which to question and speculate. There has been, too, a special reliance on the early Church Fathers, leading thinkers of the first Christian centuries who struggled long, hard, and well to define *The Faith* of the rapidly developing new religion. (See Chapter 6.)

Anglicans give prime emphasis to the Bible, having perhaps more Bible in their services than any other branch of the Church. But there is also the belief that God didn't stop revealing Himself after Jesus' Ascension into heaven or after the Bible was finalized. Anglicans are open to the further revelations of God. which came during the centuries of Christian history and still come today. *Holy Scripture* and a high place for *tradition* are accompanied by an emphasis on *reason* in the formulation and maintenance of The Faith as far as Anglicans are concerned. It is a sound, steady, comfortable, and challenging three-legged stool on which to sit.

That, roughly, is who we are, where we came from, and how we got to be. There are many good books which cover our history in detail. In most places where people travel today there are Anglican Churches. I have taken Communion in Canada, the American Cathedral in Paris, on the front lines in World War II, in a tiny chapel on a remote Caribbean island, and in Costa Rica. I have always felt welcome and that I belonged. While the services differ in some respects from country to country, the overall approach and underlying spirit are uniform. Although the *Book of Common Prayer* has now been through various revisions on national levels, I find that I can even follow the service in a foreign language I do not know.

It is said that Christendom today is in an ecumenical age, meaning a coming together of all Christians in understanding, in mutual respect and love, in learning from each other. Many see the Anglican Communion as a key in this movement, as a bridge between the Protestant denominations, Roman Catholicism, and the Orthodox Communions. There are now over 1000 separate "churches" in the United States. It would appear to be high time for an ecumenical emphasis. My personal thought is that there may never be an all-out organic union among the churches as there seems to have been in the very beginning. Given our various subcultures, I'm not sure there should be.

But we are all one in Christ. There is "one Lord, one Faith, one Baptism, one God and Father of us all!" (Eph. 4:5-6) The Episcopal Church, nationally and locally, is working toward deeper understanding and basic agreement among all practicing Christians. We are open to learning from others. In fact, we need the evangelistic zeal of Southern Baptists, more of the awareness of the Holy Spirit of the Pentecostals, more of the deep peace and acceptance of the Quakers, more of the higher mystical practices of the Orthodox, more of the solid commitment of faithful Roman Catholics, and no doubt some more of lots of things. I love my Church because we are open to these kinds of gifts.

The circle is somehow closed again when we realize that the story of the Episcopal Church, like your story and mine, is like The Story. There have been and will be wilderness wanderings, mountaintop experiences, and all the shades in between. This is so because the Episcopal story continues The Story, God's Story, as do the stories of all other Christian communions. We are all one in Him, and we go forward together in His Name and to His Glory.

6. The Faith

As distinguished from my personal faith and from yours, there is *The Faith* of the Church, inherited from the first Apostles, preserved, enriched, and interpreted by the Church. Henry VIII's title, "Defender of the Faith," was given by the Church which is, by her very nature, the chief defender of The Faith.

And The Faith needs to be, must be, defended, or else you and I in our private, little worlds, in our ignorance, in our prides and prejudices, will go off the deep end and arrive at a faith that is out-of-balance, less than whole. It may be impossible for a human being to embrace The Faith in its entirety at all times and in all places. We may sometimes veer heavily on the side of sin and away from forgiveness. Or we may get so turned temporarily toward love that we forget the place of God's law. The great body of The Christian Faith is maintained by the Church and is a corrective to our various whims, deviations, misunderstandings. And the Church is careful to keep confronting us in various ways with her articles of Faith which may be found throughout the *Book of Common Prayer,* especially in the ancient creeds and more specifically in "An Outline of the Faith," pages 845-62.

Faith itself, whether the Church's or yours and mine, is a gift from God. It seems that on our own we can't have faith very well. And it has been rightly observed that we grow in faith. We move on from one level of faith to another. The Epistle to the Hebrews defines faith as "the assurance of things hoped for, the conviction of things not seen." (Hebrews 11:1)[8] This is a powerful and helpful statement to me, worthy of much prayerful reflection.

None of us is a stranger to faith. We exercise a lot of it all the time: in other people, in elevators, in motorists not passing on hills, in airplanes. The entire method of science is based on an unproven faith in the orderliness and rationality of nature. We are used to having faith. And it is usually not blind faith.

The Church urges us not to have a blind faith in religious matters either, but a *reasonable* faith. The Church expects us to build our own faith on the basis of reason, experience, study, experimentation, sharing with others, prayer, and other such means. And the Church guides us in this by confronting us continually with The Faith in its wholeness and deep mystery, stated in power ful, symbolic language.

Few people I know have much difficulty believing in God, although they may differ in their understandings of God. To be a Christian one must also believe that God is active in His world, even though it is hardly essential to be able to spell out exactly how God is active. The best way I know to come by this faith is to examine our own stories in detail and thereby gain insights into God's actions in our own lives. Christians who pray regularly for themselves and others soon become convinced that something is happening. Archbishop Ramsey of Canterbury once said, "I don't know how prayer works, but I have noticed that when I stop praying the coincidences also stop."

Another essential to Christian Faith and practice is the belief that Jesus Christ is the Son of God, Savior of the world, God come to earth Himself in the flesh of man, the Father's chief revelation of Himself and of His will. Whether Jesus of Nazareth had this faith about Himself is another matter and the kind of proposition we might enjoy discussing sometime. What, it seems to me, is essential for Christians to believe about Jesus is:
1. God is fully in Him.
2. He was fully man.

3. He revealed God's nature and will.
4. He gave Himself for us and for our salvation.
5. God the Father raised Him from the dead.
6. He is with us now and always.

All of this is high mystery, just like life itself. Man simply cannot comprehend all that these symbols mean. In Jesus, God intervened in the affairs of the world and still does so today. Sometimes the best we can do is try to act as if we believed and say, with an early follower, "Lord, I believe, help my unbelief." And He will.

There is a kind of negative approach that may be helpful. This is to ask who or what, if not Jesus, will be my Lord? Who offers as much to me and the world? What other Lord is as proven as He, as true? It is plain, as far as I know, that there just is no other. If we want help, power, and salvation, we must commit ourselves to God's only Son.

Another helpful aid to me has been the faith of others. I have been gifted to have known fairly well a few people who seemed to me to be saintly. They were intelligent, well educated, open to new ideas, effective in living their own lives, possessed of a deep peace. It was clear they believed, and knowing this my own faith was bolstered. Like in the song *Old Time Religion,* if it was good enough for these folks I so admired, it's good enough for me.

I once heard a very learned and respected Jewish Rabbi say, "We (i.e. Jews) don't need an intermediary like Jesus. We deal with God directly." Although this scholar had attended a Christian seminary, I'm afraid he missed the point, or else he was pushing the understanding of his hearers. Jesus is not just an intermediary. He is God come to earth to give us direct, essential, indispensable help.

The movie *Oh God* is a classic portrayal of a non-Christian point of view, and it sort of confounds me that so many Christians haven't recognized this. God (played by George Burns) appears to his selected prophet (John Denver) and seeks to speak through him. God's message is, "I've given you people all you need, now get with it! Shape up and fly right. I'm going off to Africa to be with my animals. I like animals." It's a pick-yourself-up-by-your-bootstraps operation. On the other hand, God in Christ is saying, "You don't have all you need. You can't do it by yourself. I have been sent to help you, to *save* you."

There are, for sure, real differences between Christianity and some of the world's other great/religions.

The subject of exactly who and what Christ is becomes surprisingly deep and difficult once you try to come to grips with these questions for yourself. The study of this is called "christ-ology." There are many different christologies. One very prevalent one is Adoptionism. This holds that Jesus of Nazareth was so fine a person that God adopted Him as His very own son, sent His power into Him, and raised Him from the dead after He was crucified. This has its attractions to the modern mind. In seminary, as a result of a paper I wrote, one professor thought I was bordering on this view. He told me that Adoptionism would get me in trouble and that I should do some more reading and thinking.

Although I didn't fully understand what he meant, I took him at his word and kept searching. I knew from Church History that Adoptionism had been declared a heresy (an unorthodox deviation from The Faith) in the Eighth Century. I didn't have to agree with this ruling, but still, it registered with me that The Faith of the Church excludes Adoptionism. The Faith seeks to correct my errant tendencies. Since then, I have swung away from Adoptionism and am more comfortable in my faith. This is only one example of how The Faith has helped me.

My whole point in this chapter is that The Episcopal Church, along with numbers of other Christian communions, affirms and embraces The Faith of the Church as stated in the early councils, the Nicene and Apostles' Creeds, in the great traditions of Christendom, and as given to us by the first Apostles. We are an *apostolic* church which means following in the footsteps of those first Apostles. Our bishops are in direct line of succession from the Apostles. We don't hold this as "necessary for salvation," but other things being equal, we think it more than just a "nice thing" to have a bishop in *Apostolic Succession* confirm us and ordain our priests, putting them, too, in Apostolic Succession. Our bishops, priests, deacons, and laity have extra cause to defend The Faith since they are all direct heirs of the Apostles. Roman Catholics and the Orthodox Churches also have bishops in direct Apostolic Succession.

Sometimes we hear people boasting that they have their own private faith, as opposed to The Faith, and that this is fully OK. While we do each have our own individual faiths, that in my view is only all right as long as we stay open and listen to the Church's Faith. In our newly revised *Book of Common Prayer,* the Nicene Creed (Page 326) has been changed from the first person singular (I believe) to the original first person plural (We believe). This is to emphasize that the creed is stating the belief of the Church, not necessarily that of individual members. There is a difference.

It should be noted that there is a very wide latitude within The Faith. By and large, the creeds and other statements of The Faith have been put together to exclude unacceptable, unorthodox positions (heresies). They exclude more than they include. They are protections against our wandering off too far on our own and getting into a one-sided, off-balance position. Then, too, it needs to be said that the creeds and other statements of The Faith contain much symbolic language. It is important that we continually guard against our tendency to see everything as simple, literal, one-meaning signs.

A modern, respected Christian theologian, Hans Kung, has rightly cautioned that Christians need to know, indeed must know, what they want and where they stand.[9] He reminds us that Communists know clearly what they want and that non-Communisits, too, know what Communists want. This, Kung says, should also be true of Christians but often is not. What is your definition of a Christian?

Although there are other, weaker definitions, Kung's appeals most to me. He says that a Christian is a person who 1) believes Christ is who The Faith claims Him to be and 2) does all things possible to personally follow Christ and to forward His mission on this earth. Anything less than this is a watering-down of The Faith. On the other hand, this is the goal, the ideal. We are all still growing and none of us has yet attained the ideal.

It is a great comfort to me as a shield for myself, for my children, and for my congregation, that my Church gives us the mighty protection for all time of the one, holy, catholic (means "universal"), apostolic Faith of God's Holy Church, that Body of which Jesus Christ is the head and all baptized people are the members. We are protected against me and any heresies I might be espousing and against any priest or layman who strays too far in one direction or another. I know this is good for me and for my people and for all who follow. For this I am grateful. I can be confident in The Faith.

7. *The Journey*

It is unfair and untruthful to tell The Story as though it were an easy thing, full of sweetness and light, devoid of suffering and pain. The fact is that to "pick up our crosses and follow Him" is not easy in any sense of that word we commonly use. It is for sure that Christians experience increasing fulfillment, much joy, and an awareness of new things happening, but there are also frustration and disappointment, dark nights of the soul, doubting, even degrees of persecution. In looking briefly at the Christian life in this chapter, I need to begin by saying that, to my knowledge, no one has ever found it easy.

From the beginning, even in the case of our Lord himself (Luke 2:52), the Christian experience has been understood as one of growth. It has been likened to a journey, a pilgrimage - we are sojourners, strangers in the world. The religious quest is to become more and more one with God and His will. He is our true home.

It begins with a call. Jesus said, "No one can come to me unless the Father who sent me draws him." (John 6:44) As with Abraham, Moses, and many others, we are given the strength and courage to attempt tentatively to answer. By the nature of things, this call leads us eventually to the Church, His body. There, after prayer, instruction, and reflection, we are Baptized and made members of His body.

This is the sacrament of initiation. I would be hard-pressed to try to say all that it might mean. It is enough for me to believe He commanded it. I make a decision to follow Him, and so I am Baptized. I am accepted just as I am: forgiven, cleansed, empowered, and put on the road toward being one with God in and through His Son, my Lord. I make some vital promises. For details, see the service in the *Prayer Book,* page 299. You will see that it is serious business.

Just a word about infant Baptism, a source of some controversy in Christendom. This practice was begun early in the Church's history and is still followed by the majority of Christians. However, there are some major exceptions which grew out of the Reformation. Episcopalians believe Baptism is a sacrament, an outward and visible sign of inward and spiritual grace (help) and that its effectiveness does not depend on the degree of one's faith. Indeed, we feel that one cannot have enough faith to *make* it effective. It is a gift which we wish to receive. A baby has had no choice at all about being born, about who will be its parents, about what it will eat or wear, about being an American citizen, or about anything else. Its parents decide it will be put on the Christian way early in life. The parents believe this to be at least as important as its food, drink, clothing, and nationality. Godparents or sponsors take the vows for the baby and promise to see that it is raised in the Church. (Incidentally, the controversy about "sprinkling," "pouring," or "immersing" leaves me a little cold. God's Church has decreed that each of these methods fulfills the mechanical requirements of the sacrament. Episcopalians may be baptized by immersion if they wish.)

For adults, the next step, usually following immediately after Baptism, is Confirmation. Things aren't as clear as regards this sacrament. In the very early Church, adults were Baptized and then Confirmed by a bishop through the Laying on of Hands. (The biblical ground for this is in Acts 4:14-17.) Later, children, who had been Baptized as infants were Confirmed by a bishop when they reached the "age of discretion" (whatever that means). They took on for themselves the vows that had been made for them. And, not incidentally, they became a part of the

Apostolic Succession.

Much later, Confirmation became a service of induction for adults transferring into our church from other Christian communions. Since they have made a new decision which often involves a new beginning, it is surely appropriate that this important event be marked with a meaningful sacrament. The new member renews his Baptismal vows and is "confirmed" in this by a bishop, also putting the new member into the Apostolic Succession.

Confirmation, then, is a second Christian commitment accompanied by vows as in Baptism. In this sacrament, the outward and visible signs are the Laying on of Hands by a bishop and his repeating certain words. The inward grace bestowed is the increasing presence of the Holy Spirit. It is a further invitation to and an enablement of an increasingly full Christian life.

These are the initial steps and only the bare beginnings of a life-time journey. Dedication to Jesus Christ and His way are required. It would not be good to enter this path too lightheartedly. It is not a trial marriage. It is for keeps. We can be Baptized and Confirmed only once. (There is provision, however, for a reaffirmation of commitment at the time of the bishop's visitation for any who would like to do so.)[10]

The next step is crucially important, yet, many do not take it, perhaps because of lack of instruction. A spiritual discipline, appropriate to you, must be put together and faithfully followed. Without this there will be little growth, and the real possibility of slipping backward. It happens all the time. This is why I need to emphasize this point with *all the power I can muster.*

It has been observed in truth that our spiritual journeys to God are as different as snowflakes. We are all at different places, and we do not grow uniformly. There will inevitably be times of despair, frustration, and disappointment. Without a firm plan, we not only fail to grow, we falter. The second "getting lost" may be worse than the first. Because of this danger, I feel a strong obligation as a priest and pastor to caution new members carefully before they proceed.

It is strongly suggested by all who should know that we each acquire a spiritual director or guide. This can be a priest or a layman who is well along the way. Such a guide is of much help in putting together our personal plan and in helping us evaluate it as we go along, changing it as necessary. This step is done by simply asking whomever you choose to be your spiritual director, and we keep on trying until we get one. It's OK, too, to change directors from time to time, for it is entirely likely that you will outgrow your director, or you might come to want one with a different emphasis. True, most Christians we know don't have spiritual directors. That doesn't void my conviction that The Journey is much safer and more productive with one.

It is possible that the "Director" you have will take the form of a group, some like-minded people with a leader. This would be far better than no guide at all. The main point is that to my knowledge no one has *ever* made much solid progress in the spiritual life without a human companion, a guide, a mentor. Some of us try to go it alone, and this just doesn't work. Sooner or later, without direction we come to a standstill.

Your personal, spiritual plan may include such things as the following which are listed in no particular order:

1. A firm, unshakable commitment to worship God in His Church every Sunday. Whether on vacation or whatever, this would appear to be the minimum requirement of any plan. If you are sick, let your priest know and he will come to you.

2. You may want to include other Church services on a weekly or monthly basis.

3. Keep a journal of your spiritual pilgrimage. List the things you have found helpful, the problems you have, your progress or lack of it. This will be a valuable resource in lots of ways for both you and your director. Your own, detailed, personal story might be the first entry.

4. Taking Holy Communion regularly and making careful preparation. This sacrament is now generally offered by Episcopal Churches at all regular services. Like Baptism, this is a *major sacrament*.

And, like Baptism, lots could be said about it, but never everything. At the least, Christ told us to do it, and we believe He had important reasons for this command. Episcopalians believe Christ is present in a special way in the consecrated (made holy, blessed) bread and wine. At the coronation of a king, on death row, at a marriage, a birth, or a funeral, at a departing or a returning, at a beginning or an ending, it is both the most and the least that man knows to do. It is a holy mystery, essential to Christian progress.

As with all sacraments, proper preparations need to be made for Holy Communion -also called The Lord's Supper, The Holy

Eucharist (thanksgiving), and, sometimes, Mass. Your spiritual director or priest can help you plan a preparation that is suitable for you.

5. Regular prayer. This is a big subject and no attempt will be made to cover it here. All Christians I know who are serious about their journey say that prayer is essential. There are several different kinds of prayer and some will be more helpful to you than others. St. Paul instructs us to pray "constantly." There are ways to do even that when you are ready.

6. Regular study of Christian writings. The short, daily readings in *Forward Day by Day*[11] is a good place to begin. Your spiritual director can be a help there, too, in making suggestions.

7. Tithing to the Church of time, talent and money. This is not a one-way street. If you need the Church, the Church needs you just as much. It is in giving that we receive - it really is!

8. Closely akin is some kind of set offering of time and talent outside the Church. All of us are called to be ministers of the healing love of God in Christ. Grace and power from God is much like electricity flowing through a light bulb. When I turn on the switch and let God's love flow through me, I find that I am

strengthened. My own light comes on when I attempt to let God's love flow through me to others.

Some people have understood the vertical arm of the cross as pointing upward to God, signifying the relationship between the individual and God. Similarly, the horizontal arm signifies our outreach to others. The cross is not complete without both arms and neither is the spiritual life. Ministry to others in the Name of Christ can be done in many ways, but if it isn't planned, it isn't likely to happen.

9. Formal Christian Education. Adult Church School, Christian Education courses, Bible study, and the like may be a part of a spiritual discipline. One of the finest courses I know about is an extension course for local groups called "Education for Ministry -Theological Education by Extension." It is written and published by our School of Theology, University of the South, Sewanee, TN 37375. The dedicated people there will be happy to send you an outline of this course with full particulars. It is more than a "course," rather an exciting new approach to Adult Christian Education that is outstanding.

10. Prayer Groups. Although these might

be a little threatening at first, they are helpful for many people.

11. Retreats. Just as many Christians take a few minutes every day to be alone with God, many also set aside a day or two at regular intervals for a retreat. This means getting away from home and work for a quiet time with God. Your priest or spiritual advisor will be able to tell you what facilities are available for retreats in your area.

12. Use of the sacraments as needed. Our Church provides for Spiritual Healing and Private Confession. Ask about these. They are parts of the whole armor the Church provides.

There are other things—these are just idea starters. The main point is to make a plan suitable for you and not too ambitious. Stick with your plan at least three months or so, then change it if you want. Exciting ways will open before you as you grow in the life of Christ. You will be happy and surprised to see yourself changing in directions you wouldn't have imagined.

When you backslide, or slip, as most of us do, seek the help you need from your priest or other friend. God never forsakes us, always welcomes us back and strengthens us.

I love my Church because it stresses

growth, as Jesus did. When the bishop Confirmed me, he laid his hands on my head and said, "Defend, O Lord, this thy child with thy heavenly grace, that he may continue thine forever and *daily increase* in the Holy Spirit *more and more* until he comes to thine everlasting kingdom. Amen."[12] (italics mine) The emphasis is on the journey, growing in The Faith. My Church provides many helpful, proven tools for me to use as I begin and to use as I continue for as long as I live. It is an exciting, forward-looking, fulfilling journey leading to new life, new wholeness, new adventure on the mission of our Lord and Savior.

******

This is a good place to add a short note about the other sacraments of the Church, "outward and visible signs of inward and spiritual grace (help)." Baptism and Holy Communion, as I have mentioned, are the two major sacraments. Confirmation, Holy Matrimony, Absolution (forgiveness of sins), Healing, and Ordination are the five minor ones. We believe they are much more than certain words accompanied by certain actions and sometimes using certain symbols. They are power-packed, God's own chosen vehicles for our help.

8. The Environment

The Church itself is a sacrament, too - an outward and visible sign of inward and spiritual realities. This chapter will deal briefly with the outward aspects of the Church, the organization and government.

We begin with our Bishop. There can be no Episcopal Church without him (or, maybe someday, her). He is the chief pastor and top executive officer in a geographical area called a *diocese*. Tennessee has three dioceses. The Diocese at East Tennessee includes a bit of north Georgia. Florida has five or six dioceses Alabama and Georgia each have two. There are various arrangements. The Bishop may have one or more assistant Bishops. Priests who assist him are called *canons*.

Each diocese is made up of a number of congregations. Those that are self-supporting are called *parishes*. Those that aren't are *missions*. Once a year, or more often if necessary, these local churches send delegates to the *convention* of the diocese. The Bishop chairs the convention. The convention elects the Bishop and once elected, he is for keeps - until he retires. The Diocesan Convention passes the budget for the next year, elects delegates to the tri-annual national convention, elects other officers and committees, and takes on such other matters as may come before it. It elects a *Council* of *laymen* and clergy to serve with the Bishop in handling the affairs of the diocese when the Convention is not in session. In Tennessee each parish has three lay delegates to the Convention, elects other officers and committees, and takes on such other matters as may come before it. It elects a *Council of laymen* and clergy to serve with the Bishop in handling the affairs of the diocese when the Convention is not in session. The parishes and missions have lay delegates to the Convention. All the clergy in the diocese are delegates, but there are always more *lay delegates* than clerical. So, each diocese is governed by a Convention and by a Council with the Bishop as chief executive officer and also chief pastor.

Vestry elects its officers: Senior Warden, Junior Warden, Clerk, and Treasurer. The Vestry has final responsibility for the financial and material affairs of the parish. Its members see that the money is raised, approve the yearly budget and monitor the actual performance under it, make provisions for the care of the grounds, buildings, and equipment. The Vestrymen also serve on committees, provide strong leadership and support of programs, and plan for the future. They may be a council of advice for their priest. Their responsibilities are many and varied.

One of their major responsibilities is securing a priest to serve their congregation. The priest is called a *rector* if he is serving a parish and a *vicar* or *priest-in-charge* if he is with a mission. The Vestry of a congregation without a priest appoints a search committee which works closely with the Bishop. Each member of the congregation may be asked to fill in a questionnaire as the Vestry studies what qualifications they should seek in a new priest. After thorough planning, fact gathering and interviewing, the Vestry votes to issue a call to the priest of their choice, again in consultation with their Bishop. There may be further talks with the candidate. It is usual for the parish to pay the priest's salary, auto allowance, utilities, health insurance, pension assessments, and supply a suitable home called the *rectory* (in a mission: *vicarage).* There may be other benefits.

When the priest accepts the call and moves in, he becomes the spiritual head of the parish and its chief executive officer. He chairs meetings of the Vestry and appoints all committees of which he is always an *ex of-*

ficio member. He has control of the use of the church's buildings and property. He bears the same relationship to his parish as the Bishop does to the diocese. He serves under and obeys his Bishop in all spiritual matters and is actually an assistant to the Bishop who is the chief pastor of all the congregations and members. (Most Episcopal churches have a special Bishop's chair near the altar as a reminder that it is the Bishop who is really in charge and ultimately responsible.)

Once a priest becomes the rector of a congregation, an almost insoluble relationship is established. He cannot be discharged by the Vestry or the congregation, and he cannot resign without the Vestry's permission. In many ways, the relationship is like a marriage, complete with courtship, honeymoon, and trials. There must be strong mutual support and respect, good communication, and cooperation.

The rector's job is interesting, challenging, completely absorbing, and never done. As a priest, he conducts services, preaches, and administers the sacraments of the Church. As a pastor, he seeks to get to know his people and to be available to each of them. He will do some counseling, formal and informal. Teaching is one of his major responsibilities. He may get bogged down in administration unless he gets positive help from an understanding Vestry. Priests usually get a four week vacation, are encouraged to pursue continuing education goals and are permitted to serve the diocese in various ways. They may also serve the community in volunteer roles.

Candidates for the ordained ministry are carefully screened in every way, including psychiatrically. They must be approved at several different stages by their Vestry, their Rector, a committee of the diocese and by the Bishop. Most are college graduates and attend one of 11 Episcopal seminaries. This three-year course leads to a Master of Divinity degree. Then, after further testing and approvals, they are ordained *deacon* and normally serve a year in this *order* before being ordained priest. Only bishops can ordain, and only priests can be consecrated bishop. Deacons, priests and bishops are set apart for certain specific functions in the Church. Everyone, lay and ordained, is a minister and there is increasing emphasis on the ministry of the laity.

Many people are not sure what to call a priest. The title ''reverend,'' like ''honorable,'' is an adjective and is only cor rect with a "the" in front of it, as The Reverend Mr. Jones. The proper way to address him is Mr. Jones or, in some parishes, Father Jones. Also, many priests are called by their first names. A bishop is The Right Reverend. The dean of a seminary or of a cathedral is The Very Reverend.

There have recently been some new directions in what is called the non-stipendiary priesthood. These are candidates who study for the priesthood at home under a tutor while continuing their regular jobs. They must pass the same tests and evaluations as seminary-trained men and women. After ordination they usually serve a local parish on a part-time basis with no salary and continue to work at their former job. This is in the tradition of St. Paul who was a tentmaker and would take no pay from the churches he served.

Under the direction of the Vestry, each parish normally has an *Every Member Canvass* in the fall of each year. This is to secure pledges of financial support from the members for the following year. Except in emergencies, such asking for money and pledges is a once-a-year matter. Based on what the members have pledged, the Vestry makes up a budget. This includes the local operating expenses, a gift to the diocese, and probably some other outside giving. It is the practice of many of our churches to give the *open offering* (money received outside of that given as payment on pledges or otherwise designated) from one Sunday each month to their priest for his *Discretionary Fund*. The priest may spend this income in whatever way he wants, at his discretion.

The diocese operates financially in a similar way. Each congregation makes a pledge to the diocese for the next year. A diocesan budget is submitted to the annual Convention for approval. The diocese, in turn, makes a pledge to the national Episcopal Church with headquarters in New York City.

The national church is headed by a bishop called the *Presiding Bishop*. He is elected by the national *General Convention* which meets at least every three years. He is the chief executive officer nationally and administers the affairs of the church with an *Executive Council* the members of which are elected by General Convention. This Convention has two houses, a *House of Bishops* and a *House of Deputies,* the latter being made up of elected clergy and lay delegates from each of the member dioceses. Votes in the House of Deputies may be taken *by orders.* (i.e., in order to pass, a resolution must secure an affirmative vote from a majority of both the lay delegates and the clergy delegates.) In a sense, then, there are three houses with laymen having as much voice as the bishops. Such votes by orders may also be required at diocesan conventions.

The national church and the dioceses operate under a constitution and by-laws. In the church, by-laws are called *canons.* Each congregation and all clergy must pledge to abide by "the doctrine, discipline, and worship" of the Episcopal Church.

Our kind of church government is different from some others. Presbyterian churches are under a presbytery, a council of ordained ministers and lay elders having jurisdiction over a certain area. On the other hand, congregational churches, like the Baptist, are ruled completely by the local congregation. The Southern Baptist Convention is a voluntary association with no formal authority over the member congregations. At the other extreme from the congregational is the Roman Catholic system where, in effect, everyone is governed by the Pope. His word is law. The Episcopal Church is in between the two extremes - the *via media* again.

Having been an Episcopalian all my life, it meant much to me as a boy and afterwards to have known some outstanding bishops and priests. These men have been solid, loving, compassionate servants of God. They have had "the peace that passeth understanding." I think it is in large part from them that I received the gift of faith, and I am grateful for them.

It is always a great day when the Bishop comes to a local congregation for his annual visitation to Confirm, to lead the service, to preach, to be the honored guest at a reception and, probably, to meet with the Vestry. On that day the open offering is given to the Bishop's Discretionary Fund. As has been said, he is the chief pastor of his diocese. The symbol of his office is a shepherd's staff, usually very ornate and made of a precious metal. The priests are his assistants. All members are free to contact the Bishop whenever the need arises. He is always open and responsive to his people. All his priests have promised to abide happily by his judgments. (For good cause, a bishop may dissolve the pastoral relationship between a priest and a congregation. But this seldom happens.)

That is the official, basic organization. There are other structures. Chief among these is the ECW (Episcopal Church Women). There are local ECW chapters belonging to the diocesan and national organizations. The ECW operates on its own and is a strong arm of the Church at all levels. All women in the Episcopal Church are automatically members of the ECW even though they might not be active in it. There may or may not be a similar organization for men.

For young people there is the EYC (Episcopal Young Churchmen) with a diocesan organization and local chapters. Because there are educational aspects of its work, the EYC is the direct responsibility of the priest who heads all teaching. Also directly under the priest may be several other organizations. The *Altar Guild* takes good care of the altar and its furnishings. Members of the *Acolyte Guild* serve the priest at the altar, carry the cross in procession, and perform other duties. The organist, choir director, and choir are essential for full Episcopal services. *Lay Readers* and *Chalice Bearers* (pass the cup of wine at Communion) are licensed by the bishop to assist at services under the direction of their priest. Ushers help with the seating, take up the offering, and see that the services run as smoothly as possible from the standpoint of the congregation. They are the official hosts. The Church School, often under a superintendent, is a big job. There may be prayer groups, study groups, and other local organizations as well as local chapters of other national groups.

In spite of all this, the Episcopal Church does not seem to be over-organized. Everything stems from a definite need. The organizations come and go, wax and wane, as needs and opportunities change. It is a free-flowing, open arrangement.

New members, and some older ones, too, should resist the temptation to hold any part of the organization in a kind of holy awe, being reluctant to ask questions or make suggestions. There is no need for secrecy. Vestry minutes and monthly financial statements are available to any member. It is important for members to attend the annual *Parish Meeting* when reports are made and new vestrymen elected. Such a meeting is required by Canon Law and is usually held in January.

For me, the Episcopal Church has a good balance between loving episcopal authority and the democratic process, between strong spiritual leadership and necessary material considerations, between preserving valuable traditions and being open to God's new calls, between giving clergy freedom with security and providing for their discipline when necessary. It seems a wise, workable arrangement for us frail humans.

Throughout the organization, one comes across the "saints" that give it real life. In every congregation there are a number of inspired and inspiring servants of God who in their faithfulness, their love, and their commitment are like yeast in dough. No priest can operate without them nor can any congregation. They hold before us that for which we are seeking.

This brings us to the inward, spiritual side of which the outward organization is only a sign. It is God's Church, filled with the Holy spirit. We believe His will for His Church will prevail. Many times we may not see Him working. Pettiness, secular concerns, and our own hypocrisy may cloud the picture. But, come what may, Episcopalians, because of their sacramental understanding, know that the Church is much more than it seems from just its outward, visible signs. It is the Body of Christ. It is holy. It will prevail.

9. The Books

We are a *liturgical* church. This means our formal services are carefully structured and follow a set pattern. However, there is surprising freedom within the required order of service.

Throughout the Anglican Communion the liturgy is similar. This requires books, and we have three of them: *The Bible, The Book of Common Prayer,* and *The Hymnal.*

I have mentioned my suspicion that our services may incorporate more Bible than those of other branches of the Church. This will be a revelation to those who claim we don't use the Bible at all, having a prayer book instead. That is, of course, not true.

The "King James Translation" was done by the Church of England and published in 1611. Since then there have been other translations. These are necessary because the meanings of the English words continually change and scholars are learning more about the original Greek and Hebrew texts. (I should not have said "original" since all we have are copies of copies.)

What do we understand the Bible to be? There are many views in my Church, no one of which is forced on anyone. For me, the books of the Old and New Testaments were written, revised, copied, and transmitted by inspired people. They record *for the faithful* a true understanding of the relationship between God and man. The Bible contains myths (see page 32), history, law, poetry, hymns, wisdom sayings, prophecies, letters, interpretations, sales pitches, outcries of pain, teachings, and much more. Each book was written at a particular place and time, in a particular culture, to a particular audience, for a particular reason, using the language and world-view then current as well as the writing styles then in vogue. None of these circumstances are the same as today. On one hand, the Bible is complex, requiring informed open study. On the other hand, it can have profound meaning even for little children.

Over a period of many years, through use and tradition, the individual books of the Bible became for the people of God "Holy Scripture." Some of the books are more valuable than others. They are not of equal weight. Taken together they are a record of salvation history, of God's saving acts in history, of The Story (See Chapter 4). I find that The Story is very like my story, so the Bible is important in helping me come to grips with my story, my relationship to God and

His will.

Today there are many new translations and our Church reviews these carefully, authorizing most of them for use in our services. The final selection is up to the local priest. I personally prefer the *Revised Standard Version* as the best for general use in our Church.

Three specific lessons from the Bible are appointed for each Sunday: one from the Old Testament, one from the Epistles (letters) and one from the Gospels. The lessons are repeated every three years, so tri-annually we read in church just about all of the New Testament and most of the key sections of the Old. It is a sign of Christian churches coming together that several other denominations use this exact same lesson plan.

The idea of having set lessons appeals to me. As a priest, I am forced to expose my congregation to the entire Bible on a regular basis, and I am also made to come to grips with parts I might otherwise walk around. It is a good system.

In addition to three lessons, a psalm is also picked for each Sunday. Many of our prayers, anthems, and hymns contain direct quotes from the Bible. So it happens we are continuously exposed to Holy Scripture in our services, and often we aren't aware of it.

The Bible, through a kind of osmosis, becomes a living part of us.

The story of *The Book of Common Prayer* is fascinating. This volume is a true work of art. At first some people may be turned off by the idea of saying the same prayers every Sunday. There are at least two advantages to this arrangement. The prayers are so beautiful, so deep, so complete, that we are forever discovering new meanings in them. They never get old, seeming always new and alive, yet comfortably familiar. In addition, the set prayers protect my people from *my* preaching at them through the prayers, taking them on my trip. *The Prayer Book* prayers are "common" prayers, that is, held in common by all the people. They are the people's prayers, not the priest's. Too, they are much more beautiful and complete than any I could compose. In fact, when I do have to write a prayer for a special purpose, I find myself coming up with the *Prayer Book* phrases that have become a part of me.

The Book of Common Prayer was first published in 1549, the work of Archbishop Thomas Cranmer of Canterbury, England. There were several early revisions. The *American Prayer Book* came after the Revolutionary War and was substantially the same as the English book except prayers for the king and queen were not now appropriate. We pray for a president instead.

There have been a few, minor revisions of the American *Prayer Book* over the years and a major revision in 1976, after over 10 years of study by the Church at all levels. Our new 1976 book contains the beautiful services and language of our past while adding many new and helpful features. There are new services in contemporary language and much more congregational participation which emphasizes the church as a *community* of believers. Holy Communion is stressed as the Lord's Service for the Lord's Day. There are new sections for private devotions and a number of new pastoral offices for offering the Church's ministry to individuals at the key crossroads of life. To begin to know it one must experience it in depth in church and elsewhere and study it at home. (This is a helpful spiritual discipline.)

Those of us who had come to love our old 1928 Prayer Book have had some pangs about its passing. We were comfortable with the old and made a little uneasy by the new. But the new book is here to stay. Its many advances will become increasingly appreciated through use.

It is strange how we get into comfortable ruts. Even changes in the type face can be upsetting. But our God and His Church simply won't let us be. We are continually challenged, called, pushed to grow and to broaden ourselves. The new book, I am personally convinced, is superior to the old as a book of *common* prayer. Some will never feel as sentimental about it as they did the former one, but there are real dangers in being too sentimental about religious things. We worship God, not a book.

Then there is the *Hymnal* and the whole subject of music in the Episcopal Church. We have hymns from every age of the Church's history, about 600 of them. One congregation can come to know only a fraction of these. It is a continual learning process.

Many parts of our services can be sung. It is part of our tradition to use styles of singing called *plainsong* and *Anglican chanting.* These use simple tunes without metre, sort of like free verse in poetry. Psalms, songs from the Bible, and ancient Christian hymns are set to these plainsong tunes. This may seem strange at first, but it has stood the test of much time. It soon grows on you, becoming a very special treat.

Sometimes larger parts of our service are chanted in plainsong. This means singing the prayers, psalms, and other parts using basically one note with a couple of other notes added at the end of the verses. Done well, this is beautiful and moving. To chant the Lord's Prayer, for example, presents it in a whole new dimension that is very meaningful.

Our musical heritage is great, beautiful, and probably unsurpassed. It is another way of glorifying God. To use it to the full there need to be a fine organ and organist, a knowledgeable and experienced director of music, and a good, dedicated choir. Not all our congregations have these ingredients. If we don't, we keep striving. Our unmatched musical heritage is always beckoning us to high efforts. But still, whether it be the magnificent National Cathedral in Washington, D.C., or a small chapel on the Cumberland Plateau in Southeast Tennessee, the music of the Church is heard and loved as a means of expressing our love for God.

There is much to say about these three books, and I've said so little. All three are almost too deep for words. None is simple. They are inexhaustible resources. And the effect they have on our services and our entire church is profound. They give a tone of respectful order, a constant and varied setting-forth of The Story and its identification with our own stories, a sense of the very presence of God through books which in every way are clearly, in themselves, works of God. I deeply love these holy books of the Church which enable me to feel God's presence, to express myself to Him much more completely than I otherwise could, and to glorify Him in the highest ways of which man is capable. The Church, out of her vast tradition, teaches us, nurtures us through her great books.

One final note about church services. It is possible to look at any church's building or watch one of its services and pretty much determine where the emphasis is, what is central. In some denominations the Word is most important. The pulpit stands squarely in the middle. If the sermon is not "good," it is likely to be a poor service.

In the Episcopal Church the Word is important but not central. The pulpit is on one side, not in the middle. Sermons tend to be short by comparison. And the "success" of the service does not depend on the effectiveness of the sermon. This is a good thing; otherwise I would seldom lead a "successful service." Episcopal Churches can have a poor sermon and still have a meaningful service. This is because other elements are more central.

The altar, the Lord's table, is in the middle with, usually, an empty cross. He is risen! The first part of the service is devoted to the Word and to prayers. There is a break for the offertory. Then comes The Great Thanksgiving of the service of Holy Communion. The bread and wine are blessed. The people come to the altar and receive the Body and Blood of Christ. The service builds to this high point. Then there is a short prayer of thanksgiving, a blessing of the people, and the service is over. The central act that holds all the rest together is the *Communion of the People*. This is a difference, and one that appeals to me. It is a matter of emphasis, not of right or wrong.

10. The Obligations

Many prospective members want to know what specific obligations they undertake by joining the Episcopal Church. Others do not ask and do not join, even though they may attend, and I suspect this has something to do with a fear of having to serve on committees, of getting involved in organizations, and of devoting a lot of extra time which they do not have. What is the real situation? What is expected?

From at least one standpoint, there are no obligations and nothing is expected. Our total response should be one of love, having nothing to do with obligation.

Every congregation of any size has members at all levels of activity. In fact, we distinguish between "active" and "inactive" *communicants* (Confirmed members). Definitions vary from priest to priest. For me, if someone pledges or comes to church a few times a year, he or she is counted "active." If they do less than this, they are put on the inactive list, which has meaning only statistically. While we may hope and pray such members will become more active, they have this freedom to decide for themselves. We accept them where they are.

On the other hand, the Church sets forth certain standards. On page 856 of the *Prayer Book* in "An Outline of Faith," the question is asked, "What is the duty of all Christians?" The answer given: "The duty of all Christians is to follow Christ; to come together week by week for corporate worship; and to work, pray, and give for the spread of the Kingdom of God."

We have made a decision. We have made certain vows and promises. If we are serious at all about these, it follows first that we will be in church every Sunday, whether we are in town or out. We are on a mission for our Lord, and we need, at least weekly, to get new strength and food for living. Then, too, the encouragement and support we give to others by our presence is immeasurable. Coming to church is a witness to fellow members and to God. It is an outward, visible sign of inward, spiritual realities. Coming to church regularly is surely the minimum obligation. It makes no sense to join any church and then not come.

Secondly, we are to *work, pray,* and *give* for the spread of the Kingdom. Taking these in reverse order, Christian giving of money doesn't receive the emphasis it should in the Episcopal Church. We are "low key" about money. This is a serious mistake because how we use our money is probably the surest indicator of who or what are our lords. Our money is a powerful symbol of our very selves. It is ours, the result of our own labor, sweat, and care. To give to the Church is to give to Christ, to God, of ourselves. For this to have any meaning at all to anybody, including us, we must give enough to make a difference. Jesus' words, "For where your treasure is, there will be your heart also," (Mt. 6:21, Luke 12:34) are true beyond question. Many Christians have discovered for themselves our hearts indeed are where our treasure is, and if we give significantly to the Church there will our hearts be.

Prayer is a subject which requires specialized instruction and practice. Jesus prayed often and at length. He taught his disciples to pray. Without regular prayer, very few, if any, can make much progress on the Christian journey.

The work we do for the Church can take many forms. It can be in the Church organizations or outside in the world or both. The fact is if we attend church regularly, give substantially, and pray in a disciplined way, the work part will naturally follow. We won't be able to help ourselves. Appropriate ways for us to work for the Kingdom will make themselves known, and we will respond in love rather than from a sense of obligation or guilt.

Certainly the obligations we take on should only be those to which we feel called. We are free to say "No." As new members, we may try this or that, back off or come on, as we experiment to find the best way for us. We are all different and in different places. What is right for one may be wrong for another. Tragically, it sometimes happens that a new member takes on too much, gets discouraged, and becomes inactive. When asked to take on a job, whether we say "Yes" or "No," we are loved and accepted. Or we may not get asked and want to volunteer. That's OK, too. We answer the call in the best way we can.

One thing is certain: God and His Church have high expectations for each of us. We are called to be saints, but we are free to choose the paths we take and to take them in our own good time. There is no set expectation of anyone, only high hopes that in and through the Church we will each find new life, new wholeness, new health, and be a part of bringing this Good News to others. The obligations we undertake are not so much to the Church as to an entire, new life. The exact way is up to each of us.

There is another dimension that is important and is often overlooked. The Church is a community, whether we accept that fact or not. It always was and always will be. The power of the Church is in its community. We are fellow travelers. It has been shown again and again that no one can go it alone. I need you, and you need me. We both need our privacy, too, But we need each other as we go forward under Christ.

Our chief service is called Holy *Communion* - communion with God and with each other. It is both a private and a corporate act. In Chapter 7 I wrote about The Journey and suggested some ways that have been found helpful. There will be no journey if we try to do it alone. Fellowship, love, and communion are necessary. For this to happen, there needs to be both structure and effort.

The Church's organizations are one means to this end. For example, members of the Altar Guild perform a quiet and needed service. But in the doing of it they come together as friends in the service of their Lord. This is true of all the organizations, or should be. They are more than they seem. They, too, are outward and visible signs of inward, spiritual realities. From a practical standpoint, not from obligation, we must be involved to some extent with the people of the Church for the health of our own soul and for theirs.

Here is perhaps the crux of the matter, "and for theirs." "As you did it to one of the least of these my brethren, you did it to me." (Mt. 25:40) It is in giving that we receive. This is the backbone, the heart of Jesus' teaching and of His life. If we are to follow Him seriously, as we promise to do at Baptism and Confirmation, we have to give of ourselves.

Many of us think we have very little to give. We have a low view of ourselves. The Church teaches otherwise: we are all children of God, created in His image. I am reminded of a little hymn in the children's section of *The Hymnal:*

> How can I repay thy love,
> Lord of all the hosts above?
> What have I, a child, to bring
> Unto thee, thou heavenly King?
>
> I have but myself to give:
> Let me to thy glory live;
> Let me follow day by day
> Where thou showest me the way.[13]

All is not smooth sailing, of course. The Church has people for members, and people are sinners. None of us is perfect. There will be personality conflicts, real and imagined hurts. We are taught there are three responses to conflict: fight, flight, and faithfulness. As followers of Christ, we are most of all to be faithful as He is faithful. We are to be faithful to Him and to His Church come what may. When "the roll is called up yonder" I am convinced it is for our faithfulness we will be judged. It seems to me to be the only true measure of success and failure in the Christian way.

In all of this, the special emphases of the Episcopal Church play a part. We are a Church of love rather than law, of forgiveness rather than discipline, of freedom under Christ rather than restrictions, of helpfulness rather than censure, and of a high sense of the worth of every individual. Being our true selves and being comfortable with this are major goals.

Summing up about obligations, there are no hidden ones. Obviously there are things that need to be done, if the Church is going to continue to function as it has with choir, ushers, vestry, teachers, evangelists, grass cutters, dusters, lay ministers, and all the rest. If there are not people to do these things, they just don't get done. Still, by joining the Church no one agrees to do anything other than follow Jesus Christ as Lord and Savior. The only solid commitments asked for are those in the service of Holy Baptism (Page 299), and these are enough. If you still have reservations, talk openly and fully with the priest of your local Episcopal Church.

11. The Stepping Stones

As I come to the end of this little book about the Church I love, there are a few other points that should be mentioned. I am calling these "stepping stones" because they have been important helps for me and for many along the way ... guides, signposts that make things easier.

1. *The Church Year.* The vast majority of Christians across the world observe the Church Year. It goes round and round from year to year, but, like those "Slinky" coiled-spring toys, as you go round and round, you also go up and up (or deeper and deeper). Each cycle is different for us because each of us is always at a different place.

The Church Year has six seasons: *Advent, Christmas, Epiphany, Lent, Easter, and Pentecost. Advent* is the four weeks before Christmas. With purple as its color, this season is meant to be a quiet time of preparation, which is hard to accomplish since our culture gets so geared up for Christmas. But the Church asks us to slow down, to think, to watch and wait expectantly - to get ourselves ready.

It is said that Roman Catholics emphasize Good Friday, the Orthodox stress Easter, and

Anglicans especially cherish *Christmas*. Be that as it may, there is no question but that for Episcopalians the late service on Christmas Eve has a very high place. The stops are all pulled. The colors flow. Warmth abounds. And Christmas lasts 12 days! The chief color is white for a high feast.

Epiphany follows Christmas, and its color is green. The themes deal with how God showed Himself to man in Jesus of Nazareth. The Feast of The Epiphany, always January 6, celebrates the coming of the Wise Men and the world-wide mission of this Jewish baby. The chief symbol is light - the light of the star, the Light of the world, the Light shining in the darkness. This season is about who Jesus is and what He does. Sometimes lasting as long as nine weeks, Epiphany's length depends on whether Easter is early or late.

Lent is the 40 days before Easter, not counting Sundays. Going back to purple, the mood is one of quietness. Like Advent, it is a time of preparation, of examination, of getting ready. There are often special additions to the Church's program: extra services, teaching series, etc. We are given opportunity and encouragement to make this season different and special. For example, this is the best time for a retreat, for a special spiritual discipline, a special offering. Ordinarily, weddings and other festive events are postponed until Lent is over. This is a time for fasting rather than feasting. The last week, Holy Week, receives special emphasis.

Then comes the mighty festival of *Easter*. This season begins on Easter Day and lasts for 50 days, one-seventh of the year. Sunday is to the week what Easter is to the year. As at Christmas, the color is white, and we do our best to celebrate our Lord's resurrection in the best way we know. It is a joyous, bright time, contrasting sharply with the sombre tones of Lent. Many of our congregations have a special service on Easter Eve.

The Day of *Pentecost* (meaning "50 days") celebrates the birthday of the Church, the gift of the Holy Spirit to the first Christians (Acts 2). The color is red for the Holy Spirit. The next Sunday is Trinity Sunday, the only one named for a doctrine (see below). After that we enter the long season of Pentecost which lasts through the summer and into the late fall. The color is green. The emphasis now is on living the Christian life, on The Journey, The Faith, on being a disciple, on being the Church, on growing in grace.

Living the Church Year is like walking on a never-ending rug which is always coming new from the loom. Sometimes one color predominates, sometimes another, but all are always there. As we travel this ever-changing road, we are helped, enlivened, opened to growth. The changes in pace and mood get our attention. Developed over many centuries of Christian practice, and still changing, the Church Year is deeply loved by the many who set out to follow it faithfully.

2. *The Doctrine of The Trinity.* Doctrines are not very interesting until they are experienced in life. This doctrine means simply that God the Father, God the Son, and God the Holy Spirit are one God...three in one, one in three. Not too exciting.

That is, not too exciting until it is lived. I'll give just one example. Recently Lynn (my good wife) and I went to Costa Rica, partly vacation and partly Church business. The Diocese of Tennessee and the Church in Costa Rica were planning a kind of special relationship for a few years. Our trip there was a first-step, get-acquainted kind of gesture. Not knowing anything at all about this tiny country, just north of Panama, I would have chosen another spot to vacation. But circumstances were calling us to go there.

In thinking about our trip beforehand, I became more aware than usual of our belief that *God the Father* created me and the Costa Ricans and all else that is. We are one in our roots and in our heavenly Father, but our original oneness has been lost.

I kept thinking that *God the Son* calls us to be one again (John 17). We are called *by* Him to be one *in* Him. His followers give themselves to this end, as He did. This is largely what He is about.

I believe in Him. I hear His call. I want to answer. In spite of probable culture shock, language barriers, dislike of Americans, and all the rest, He whom we follow so calls us. Our Costa Rican trip, seen as an answer to the call of God the Son, became a whole new ball game. The prospects brightened. There was new excitement. My expectations about a vacation had never been like that before.

But there were some real fears. I didn't know how we would be received and had no idea at all what we could do or say. My usual compulsive tendency to have everything overplanned was frustrated by lack of information. We had, like Abraham, literally to go to a land we knew not of. And this is a little scary, even if a bloody revolution hadn't been going on in nearby Nicaragua (which it was).

At some point I suddenly became aware

of the third Person of the Trinity, *God the Holy Spirit.* I am taught that He is God's special power. He will guide, strengthen, teach, empower. Of what am I afraid? All the bases are covered. Living in this faith, we felt a new confidence.

So we went to Costa Rica consciously living out the Doctrine of the Trinity. It was probably the most unusual, memorable, and life-giving experience we have ever had. And it's not over: a trip made in the power of the Trinity may never be over.

This understanding, of God the Father who made us, of God the Son who calls us to be one, and of God the Holy Spirit who gives us what we need, can be lived out in any relationship: husband-wife, parent-child, teacher-student, employer-employee, everywhere. I have learned this from my Church. God is a triune God: three in one, and one in three. It is pure power for the good life.

Again, this is not just an Episcopal doctrine. But we, like many others, give it a high place.

3. *The Communion of Saints.* "Saints" means "Christians." The Church teaches that Christians have a special spiritual relationship with all other Christians, both those

living in this world and in the next. This, too, is not just Episcopal.

When I read St. Paul's letters, his joys and his angers, his defenses and his attacks, his victories and his disappointments, I feel that he is not only alive but is somehow one with me and all the rest of us in the Communion of Saints. In this living Communion with me are also Archbishop Cranmer who wrote the *Prayer Book,* St. Peter who, like me, had ups and downs, Jesus' mother Mary who is a model of faith, humility, and gratitude. My father, who died when I was a senior in high school, is there, along with Stephen, the first martyr, and many others. It is a glorious company of which even I am a part.

Some of these men and women are remembered on special days in the Church. But the ones we remember in this way are only the leading edge of the living company of saints of which we are all a part. This understanding, which is stressed in my Church, is another of the things that I love and that means much to me.

4. *Membership.* I have touched on this briefly before. A membership in the Anglican Communion of the one, holy, catholic, apostolic Church is a passport of welcome

throughout the world. (I particularly experienced this on a visit to the American Cathedral in Paris during World War II on a 48-hour leave from the front and more recently in Costa Rica.).

When you move from place to place it is good to ask the former priest to transfer your membership to your new parish. It is easily done and is no problem for anyone. Incidentally, if you don't, you will no longer be counted since you will go on the inactive list in your old parish. It is important to belong to the Church where you are. This is a sacrament, an outward and visible sign of your commitment, love, and support of God's Church in the place where you happen to be. If you don't transfer, this is also an outward, visible sign of something real.

On the flip side of this proposition is the circumstance when a member asks to be taken off the rolls altogether, as though this were just a social club or some such. We do not transfer people off the rolls once they are members, just like we don't get unborn. It is for keeps - and I like that.

5. *Ritual.* This word refers to the things we do and how we do them - the physical acts. When you first visit an Episcopal service you may be struck by certain actions which

might seem strange and rather odd. Ritual differs from one parish or mission to another and from one person to another.

For example, it seems usual for most Episcopalians to kneel and say a prayer when they first enter the church and again just before they leave. This isn't required and not everyone does. It is a special act that has meaning for those who do it. Some people cross themselves at certain times - an outward and visible sign with inner meaning. When understood, such acts as these can be helpful for some.

It is customary for us not to talk much in church. Most of us kneel to pray, stand for praise, and sit for instruction - but you don't have to and not everybody does.

There are a number of other such things. Everyone is invited to say "amen" at the end of prayers making each prayer his own. Many bow their heads when the cross passes in procession, and some bow to the altar when they enter or leave a pew. If the act has no meaning for you, it should not be done. But understood and having meaning, such acts can be helpful.

These and other "stepping stones" are proven aids that have evolved over the years. They deepen and enrich our life in The Faith.

12. The Experience

Just one more thought, probably the most important. What I have written about the Church I love, The Need, The Language, The Story, The Roots, The Faith, The Journey, The Environment, The Books, and the rest cannot be understood or appreciated unless experienced. They simply can have no real meaning, either positive or negative, until they have been lived. It is like no one can know about love until he has both loved and been loved. The word "hot" has to be experienced at gut level to be known. The Land of Oz, Narnia, and Bali Hai are only dreams until one has been there.,

And so it is with God and His Church. All the sacraments and symbols have to do with *real* things. The Church isn't playing games. It is for *real*. God is for *real*. His actions in this world, in our lives are for *real*. Jesus Christ is for *real*. But no one of us can possibly appreciate these facts until he or she has had experience of them.

Fortunately, if we are starting from scratch or have in some way been turned off before, a number of things seem to combine to point us in the direction of God and His Church. To start with, we are basically unfulfilled, unfinished, frustrated - our lives lack true meaning and direction. Like in The Story, we need help. So, in various ways, God calls us; this is certainly *real*. We can try to turn off the call, but it keeps coming. This is one significant pointer that leads us to suspect that God and His Church are for real.

Another is the great cloud of witnesses, the hundreds and hundreds of thousands who have experienced for themselves the things I have been trying to describe. If you haven't experienced these things yourself, you must know that many people have. This involves all kinds of people: rich and poor, educated and uneducated, nuclear scientists and day laborers, the sick and their medical doctors. They come from all walks of life, all professions, everywhere. They are not to be denied. They have something that others simply don't. I have mentioned the effect that bishops and some priests have had on my own religious life. These witnesses are for *real*. They lead us to believe that the source of their peace and strength is also for *real*. This is surely another powerful pointer or indicator.

There is another that has had particular meaning for me. In my second job after college, I worked for 10 years in the sales department of a company that manufactured and marketed over-the-counter medicines. One of these was a very old tonic for women. And, though it was in an old-fashioned bottle and carton, it sold very well throughout the country.

In the middle 50's, the research department of that company began to work on this tonic, trying to see what made it tick, or if it really ticked at all. It was made by percolating alcohol over an herb, like making coffee, and many drugs were dissolved from the herb into the alcohol. The chemists separated out lots of these drugs, identified them, and tested them separately. Lo and behold: one day they discovered that this "brew" contained an extremely potent and good drug. The old, old women's tonic had real power in it, medically proven, absolutely scientific.

Then I remember reading later an article in a trade journal about the great number of old remedies that modern science had shown to contain important drugs. The heart drug rauwolfia is one of these.

Isn't the Church somewhat like that? It is very old. Sometimes it seems old fashioned and out of date. It may appear that the original message of Jesus has been so covered up with doctrines and later interpretations as to have been seriously changed or even lost. We may conclude the Church meets only social needs for hypocrites. We may, in our lack of experience, conclude lots of things.

But the Church has lasted for 20 centuries. The very age of the Church and its continued good health point to the fact that it is for *real*. Many make fun of it, as they did the tonic for women. But they stop making fun when they discover the truth. Each person has to make the discovery for himself. For me, the very age and present vitality of the Church is a pointer that cannot be denied.

And so ends my beginning. That is all it is meant to be, that is all it is. You have nothing to lose (but the world and your life to gain) by simply giving it a try. For further information feel free to ask any member of The Episcopal Church, or simply call one of the Episcopal parishes listed in the Yellow Pages of the phone book. Ask for the rector. You will incur no obligation, and you will be treated kindly.

Of course, the Episcopal Church is not the only way by a long shot. It is just that for me and for lots of others I know and respect the Episcopal Church has made God real, the Church real, Jesus Christ real, the Holy Spirit real. In the process, we have found that it makes each of us more real, too, and our lives more meaningful. And as we see ourselves being changed, we find that the needs that brought us and have kept us here are being met. It is then that we find the experience is *real*.

Notes

1. *The Book Of Common Prayer* (1979), The Church Hymnal Corporation, New York, and The Seabury Press.
2. Used by permission. See acknowledgments.
3. *Book of Common Prayer,* p. 337.
4. *ibid.,* p. 854.
5. From The Very Rev. Urban T. Holmes, Dean, School of Theology, University of the South, Sewanee, Tennessee. Used by permission.
6. Yahweh is one translation of the Old Testament name of God given to Moses at the burning bush (Exodus 3:14).
7. The *Prayer Book,* p. 24, suggests the year 304 for St. Alban's martyrdom. However, recent correspondence with The Cathedral and Abbey Church of St. Alban's in England indicates a preference for 209.
8. All Bible quotations herein are from the *Revised Standard Version of the Bible* copyrighted 1946, 1952©, 1973 by the Division of Education and Ministry of the National Council of the Churches of Christ. Used by permission.

9. Used by permission. See acknowledgments.
10. *Book of Common Prayer* (1979), p. 310.
11. Short daily meditations based on Bible readings from Forward Movement Publications, 412 Sycamore Street, Cincinnati, Ohio 45202.
12. *Book of Common Prayer* (1928), p. 297.
13. Used by permission. See acknowledgments.

Index

Index

Index

Index

(continued from back cover)

... on and on it could go. But it always ends up at the same place: an active churchman all his life!

Bill Patten (his family and old friends call him Billy) has experienced about all of life there is, at all levels. On the surface, his story seems disorganized and disconnected. But underneath there has been one, powerful, unifying force: his love for the Church, for God, and for God's people. Believe it or not, this was the motivation for his ending a highly successful career as a top national sales executive and becoming a new car dealer. It's no wonder he finally answered his long-time urge to become an ordained priest. All else was preparation.

Since seminary, he has served congregations in Martin and Paris, Tennessee, in Ft. Oglethorpe, Georgia, and currently in Chattanooga. These were small, mission churches. Three of them became self-sustaining parishes while he was there. And in two he had a hand in new church buildings.

Bill has served three years on the Bishop and Council of the Episcopal Diocese of Tennessee and has worked in other areas of his Church. He is especially interested in the